PowerKiDS
Readers

AMERICAN SYMBOLS
SÍMBOLOS DE AMÉRICA

THE LIBERTY BELL

LA CAMPANA DE LA LIBERTAD

Joe Gaspar
Traducción al español: Eduardo Alamán

PowerKiDS
press.

New York

Published in 2014 by The Rosen Publishing Group, Inc.
29 East 21st Street, New York, NY 10010

First Edition

Editor: Amelie von Zumbusch
Book Design: Colleen Bialecki   Traducción al español: Eduardo Alamán

Photo Credits: Cover Racheal Grazias/Shutterstock.com; p. 5 DC Productions/Photodisc/Thinkstock; pp. 7, 13, 17 Superstock/Getty Images; pp. 9, 15, 21 Visions of America/Universal Images Group/Getty Images; p. 11 Mark Krapels/Shutterstock.com; p. 19 Spirit of America/Shutterstock.com; p. 23 Don Murray/Getty Images News/Getty Images; p. 24 idea for life/Shutterstock.com.

Library of Congress Cataloging-in-Publication Data
Gaspar, Joe.
 The Liberty Bell = La Campana de la Libertad / by Joe Gaspar ; translated by Eduardo Alamán. — First edition.
   pages cm. — (Powerkids readers: American symbols = Símbolos de América)
 English and Spanish.
 Includes index.
 ISBN 978-1-4777-1207-8 (library binding)
 1. Liberty Bell–Juvenile literature. 2. Philadelphia (Pa.)—Buildings, structures, etc.—Juvenile literature. I. Alamán, Eduardo translator. II. Gaspar, Joe. Liberty Bell. III. Gaspar, Joe. Liberty Bell. Spanish. IV. Title. V. Title: Campana de la Independencia.
 F158.8.I3G3718 2014
 974.8'11—dc23
                              2012046770

Websites: Due to the changing nature of Internet links, PowerKids Press has developed an online list of websites related to the subject of this book. This site is updated regularly. Please use this link to access the list: www.powerkidslinks.com/pkras/bell/

Manufactured in the United States of America

CPSIA Compliance Information: Batch #S13PK4: For Further Information contact Rosen Publishing, New York, New York at 1-800-237-9932

CONTENTS

CONTENIDO

This is the **Liberty Bell**.

Esta es la **Campana de la Libertad**.

It is old.

Es muy vieja.

It is big.

Es grande.

It is in Philadelphia, Pennsylvania.

Se encuentra en Filadelfia, Pensilvania.

It was made in England.

_____

Fue construida en Inglaterra.

It is mostly **copper**.

Esta hecha, principalmente, de **cobre**.

Its old name is the State House Bell.

La Campana de la Libertad fue conocida como la vieja campana del Estado.

It has a **crack**.

Tiene una **grieta**.

19

It is rung two days a year.

La campana se hace sonar dos veces al año.

21

You can visit it.

Tú puedes visitarla.

WORDS TO KNOW/
PALABRAS QUE DEBES SABER

copper
(el) cobre

crack
(la) grieta

Liberty Bell / (la)
Campana de la Libertad